The Klutz Book of
Balloon
Twisting

by Karen Phillips

KLUTZ®

KLUTZ®

creates activity books and other great stuff for kids ages 3 to 103. We began our corporate life in 1977 in a garage we shared with a Chevrolet Impala. Although we've outgrown that first office, Klutz galactic headquarters remains in Palo Alto, California, and we're still staffed entirely by real human beings. For those of you who collect mission statements, here's ours:

CREATE WONDERFUL THINGS · BE GOOD · HAVE FUN

WRITE US We would love to hear your comments regarding this or any of our books. We have many!

KLUTZ®

450 Lambert Avenue, Palo Alto, CA 94306

Book and all components manufactured in Taiwan.

Distributed in the UK by Scholastic UK Ltd Westfield Road, Southam, Warwickshire England CV47 ORA

Distributed in Australia by Scholastic Australia Customer Service PO Box 579, Gosford, NSW, Australia 2250

ISBN-10: 1-59174-674-4

ISBN-13: 978-1-59174-674-4

4 1 5 8 5 7 0 8 8 8

VISIT OUR WEBSITE You can check out all the stuff we make, find a nearby retailer, request a catalog, sign up for a newsletter, e-mail us, or just goof off! **www.klutz.com**

Contents

You are the BOSS of your balloons

Twisting balloons for the first time makes some people a little timid. Nervous, even.

Relax.

Once you start messing around with them, you'll be amazed how much twisting, tugging, and folding balloons can withstand. And how easy it is to make them into something wonderful. Your balloon wand may look less than perfect to you, but hand it to a kid and suddenly it becomes really and truly magical.

Why be nervous? The worst that can happen is a balloon will pop. If it does, you've got a golden opportunity for comedy.

"And that's how you blow up a balloon!"

"I knew you were a sharp kid!"

"Did you get a bang out of that one?"

Yes, it's corny. But you can get away with a lot when you're the balloon twister.

What you get

- **40 balloons**
  (8 different colors)
- **a balloon pump**

Stuff you'll need

- scissors
- a marker pen
- a little time to practice

About the Balloons

This book comes with enough balloons to get you started twisting. When you're ready to twist balloons for a party or something, you'll want to get more.

These balloons are called "260s" — because when they are inflated, they are about 2 inches (5 cm) in diameter and 60 inches (1.5 m) long.

You can get more of the balloons that came with this book from Klutz (see the inside of the back cover). You should also be able to find 260s at your local party supply store or online. Qualatex is a good brand to look for.

When a balloon pops (and it will happen), pick up all the bits of exploded balloon. It can be unhealthy if kids or animals try to eat them.

ANATOMY *of a* BALLOON

nozzle

tail

Pretty simple, huh?

Blowing Up a Balloon

Don't try to inflate one of these long balloons with lung power.
Only balloon-twisting professionals can do that.
Trust us. Use the pump.

1 Read the project instructions
to find out how much to inflate
the balloon.

2 Pull the nozzle of the balloon
over the tip of the pump.
Hold it in place just above
the rolled edge.

Use your other hand to pump
the balloon up until there is
just the right amount of
uninflated tail at the end.

Tying the **knot**

The idea is to tie a knot as close to the nozzle as possible, so you don't waste any twisting space.

Your knot should look like this...

...not this.

If you already have a comfortable method of knot-tying that doesn't waste much balloon, you can skip this part.

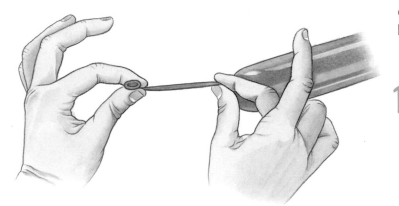

1 After inflating the balloon just enough for your project, release enough air so you can stretch the nozzle 2–3 inches (about 7 cm). Pinch with your thumb and middle finger right where the inflated part starts.

2 Loop the nozzle around your index finger so the balloon makes an X shape below your finger.

3 Push the nozzle through the gap at the top of the X.

4 Pull your index finger out of the loop and let the knot close on itself.

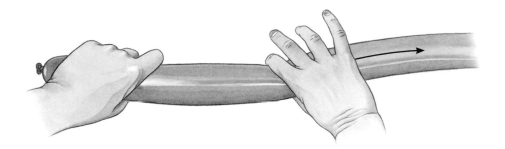

One last thing before twisting:
Stretch the balloon from the nozzle to the tail by pulling it through your grasp. Don't skip this step — it really helps.

Sword

You Need

- 1 balloon in a swashbuckling color

1 Fill the balloon nearly all the way so there is a scant quarter inch (.6 cm) of uninflated tip. Tie the balloon off and stretch it (pages 8-9).

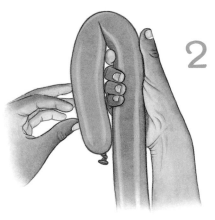

2 Grip the balloon lightly near the nozzle end and fold it over your four fingers. The nozzle should end up just over an inch (2.5 cm) below your grip.

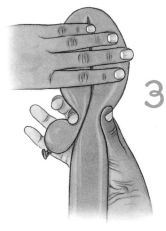

3 Squeeze both sides of the fold about an inch (2.5 cm) up from the nozzle and twist three times...

...so you end up with a loop and a round bubble.

4 Make another round bubble. Twist it three times and keep hold so it doesn't untwist.

This bubble and this bubble should be about the same size.

5 Make another loop the same size as the first one. Squeeze both sides of the base of the loop and twist them together three times.

6 Mush the parts around so the loops are on the same side...

...and pull the long end through the loops until the blade is the perfect length for your buccaneer. It can be tricky to get the blade through the loops. Just be patient and keep working at it. You'll get it.

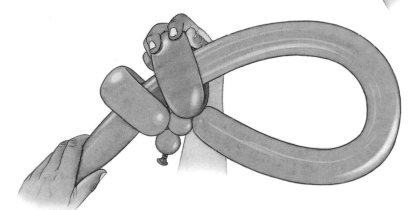

Finally, if necessary, straighten the blade by stretching it (page 9).

You Need

- 1 balloon
- a willing kid's waist

1 Fill the balloon nearly all the way so there is a scant half inch (1.25 cm) of uninflated tip. Tie it off and stretch it (pages 8-9).

Wrap the balloon around the willing kid's waist.

2 Let the nozzle end overlap by about an inch (2.5 cm) just where the balloon meets around the waist.

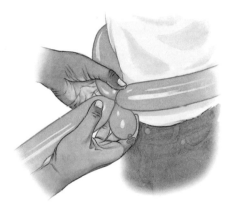

Pinch all the layers together and, with your other hand, twist both ends three times. Think of the balloon ends as a crank and the kid as a giant wind-up toy.

3 To lock the twist, push the small bubble through the center of the belt so the nozzle points to the ground.

4 Form a loop with the long end. Leaving about an inch (2.5 cm) free at the tail, squish together all the layers where they join.

5 Twist the loop three times — again, like your kid is a big wind-up toy. Push the new small bubble through the center of the belt to lock the twist.

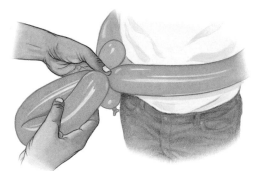

6 Arrange the belt so one small bubble is on top, one is on the bottom, and the loop sticks out to the side. Let your buccaneer slide a sword through the loop and stand back!

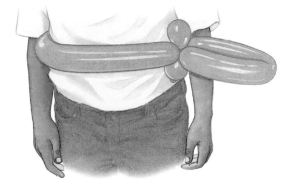

En Garde!

Basic Helmet

All by itself, the Basic is just like it sounds — stylish enough for just about any occasion. But it's also the starting point for the three cool hats to follow: the Screwball, the Viking Helmet, and the sssssstylish Snake.

You Need

- 1 balloon
- a kid with a head you can borrow

1 Fill the balloon just enough so there is no uninflated tip, tie it off, and stretch it (pages 8-9). At the nozzle end, twist three times to form a round bubble. Keep hold so the bubble stays in place.

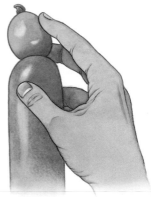

2 Wrap the bubble end around the nearest head that needs a hat.

Note where the twist overlaps the balloon.

Resist the shortcut of sizing the hat on your own head. It seems like it should work but, usually, it doesn't.

3 Take the balloon off the head. Twist the bubble together with the balloon three times — right at the spot where they overlapped.

4 Lock the twist by pushing the bubble through the loop back to its original position. You've just formed the hat band.

5 At the tail end, twist three times to form another round bubble.

6 Bring the bubble down inside the hat band, forming an arch.

Wrap the bubble around the hat band so it stays securely in place.

7 Find the center of the arch by pushing the two round bubbles toward each other. Line up the bottom ends of the arch and make sure both sides are even. Note where the balloon bends — that's the center.

Make a twist at the centerpoint by rotating one side of the arch. Twist three times.

And that's the Basic Helmet.
Read on to learn how to go way beyond basic.

SCREWBALL Hat

You Need

- a Basic Helmet (page 18)
- 1 or more balloons to curl

1 Fill a balloon just enough so there is no uninflated tip, tie it off, and stretch it (pages 8-9).

Holding the nozzle end, wrap the balloon around your arm and press it against your body. Use your other hand to manhandle the wrapped balloon, pinching the curves and squeezing it here and there. This handling, along with your body heat, will set the curl. When you take the balloon off your arm, it should have a nice loopy look.

2 At the nozzle end of your curly balloon, twist three times to make a round bubble. Wrap the bubble around the twist in the center of the arch of the Basic Helmet.

You could be done right here and have an awesome hat, or you can add more curly balloons in exactly the same way. How many? We leave that to your own sense of taste and discretion.

VIKING HELMET

You Need

- a Basic Helmet (page 18)
- 1 balloon for horns

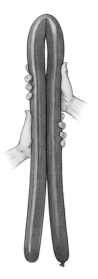

1 Fill the balloon just enough so there is no uninflated tip, tie it off, and stretch it (pages 8–9).

Find the center by lining up the two ends and walking your hands the length of the folded balloon to the bend.

2 Twist three times right at the bend. Keep hold so it doesn't untwist.

3 Run the long balloon inside the arch of the Basic Helmet so the two center twists line up.

Crisscross the halves of the long balloon so the right end is on the left, and the left end is on the right. Simple!

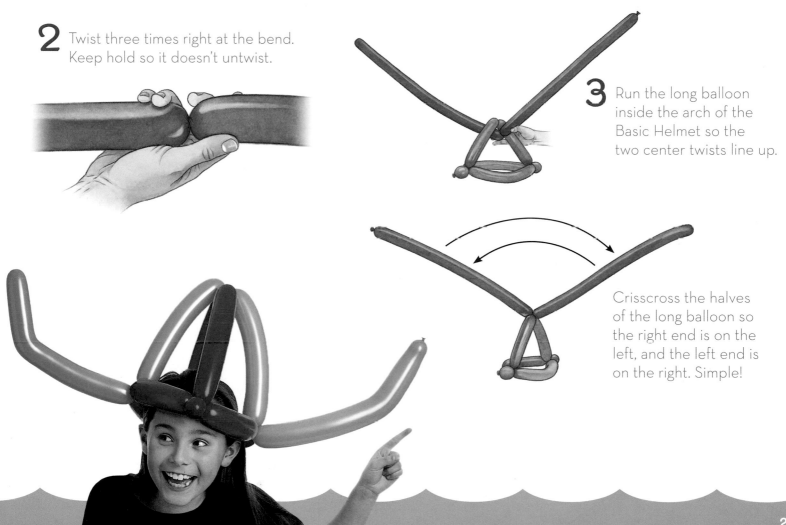

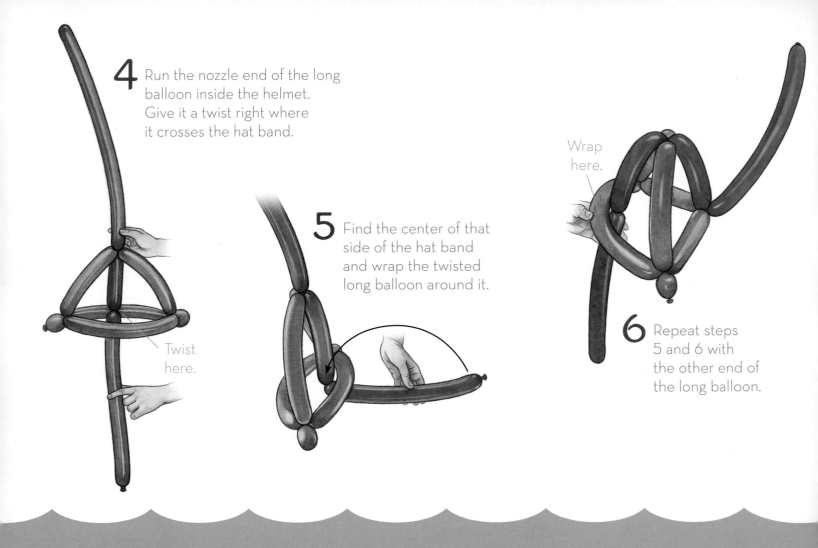

4 Run the nozzle end of the long balloon inside the helmet. Give it a twist right where it crosses the hat band.

Twist here.

5 Find the center of that side of the hat band and wrap the twisted long balloon around it.

Wrap here.

6 Repeat steps 5 and 6 with the other end of the long balloon.

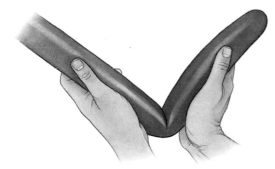

7 Now bend and roll the horns to get that nicely curved look. You may have to rotate the horns for maximum symmetry.

fierce!

Snake Hat

You Need

- a Basic Helmet (page 18)
- 1 balloon for the body
- 1 balloon for the tongue
- a marker pen

1 Fill the body balloon so there is just about an inch (2.5 cm) of uninflated tip, tie it off, and stretch it (pages 8–9).

Twist the balloon about 2 inches (5 cm) down from the nozzle to form a slightly oblong bubble.

2 Fold the bubble tight against the balloon. Pinch the tied-off nozzle together with the balloon...

...and twist three times to make a connected, matching bubble.

Push the nozzle between the two bubbles to lock them in place.

3 This is the tricky part: Grab a bubble in each hand. Hold one still and twist the other *away from you* a couple times. This is going to feel really weird and wrong. But trust us! You can do it and nothing terrible is going to happen. Go ahead — twist.

These are the snake's eyes.

4 About 4 inches (10 cm) below the eyes, fold the balloon. Squeeze both sides of the balloon right where the eyes are connected, and twist three times.

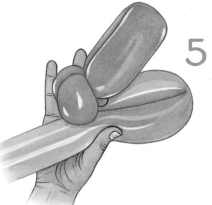

5 Make a loop that is the same size as the loop you just made. Squeeze at the base of the loop and twist three times.

This is the snake's mouth.

6 Inflate the tongue balloon a tiny bit and tie it off. Squeeze at the nozzle end to flatten it a little.

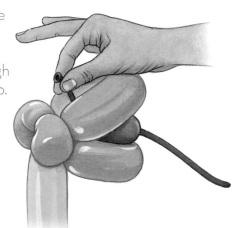

7 Set the tongue, nozzle first, in the mouth. Stretch the tied-off end and pull it through the upper mouth loop. Wind it randomly around and between the mouth and eyes to lock it in place.

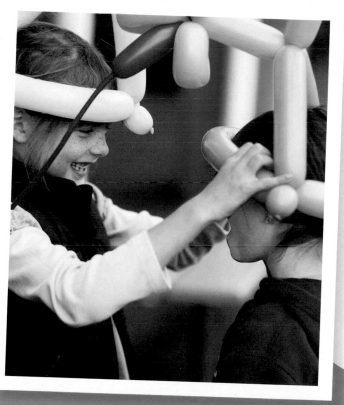

8 Use your marker to draw pupils on the eyes. It's amazing how much personality two simple dots bring to the party.

9 Now bend the head back against the body, so the tongue is pointing up to the sky. Use your whole hand to pinch the bend a few times. There should be a snapping noise as you release the pinch. After a few snaps, the balloon should stay nicely bent.

Add a few more bends along the length of the snake as you see fit.

10 Slide the snake under the arch of the Basic Helmet. Line up the arch's center twist with the first bend behind the snake's head.

Wrap the snake around the twist.

Ssssssplendid!

Flower Bracelet

You Need

- 1 balloon for the petals
- 1 balloon for the center and wristband
- scissors

1 Fill the petal balloon, leaving about 4 inches (10 cm) uninflated, tie it off, and stretch it (pages 8–9).

2 Make a fold about 3 inches (7.6 cm) below the nozzle.

Pinch the tied-off nozzle and the balloon at the base of the loop...

...and twist three times.

Push the nozzle through the loop to lock it in place.

3 Make four more petals the same way: Fold the balloon, pinch the base of the loop, and twist.

It's okay if your loops aren't all exactly the same size. Real flower petals don't match each other perfectly either.

4 You have five petals on the end of a fat stem. Now scramble the petals, making sure every petal switches places with another at least once. Once your flower is really mixed up, use scissors to cut a slit in the uninflated tip of the tail, deflating the stem.

If there isn't any uninflated tip left, pinch the air out of the very end and snip it there. No air = no pop!

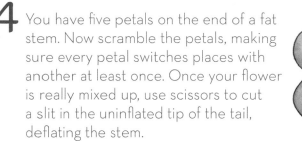

5 Wrap the deflated stem in the flower, winding randomly between the petals.

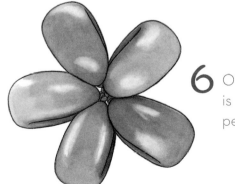

6 Once the entire stem is used up, smush the petals into a circle.

7 Blow up the other balloon just a smidge and tie it off. It should be about the size of a walnut.

8 Set the balloon, nozzle first, in the center of the flower. Stretch the tied-off nozzle and wind it between the petals the same way you wrapped the stem.

9 Take the long, uninflated tail and pull the part closest to the bubble down snug through the center of the flower. Randomly wind it between a few petals for security.

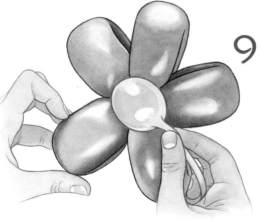

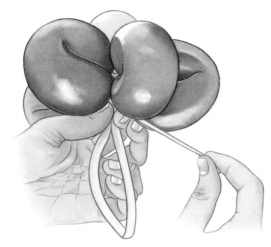

10 To form the wristband, make the tail into a big loop, leaving about an inch (2.5 cm) free at the end. With one hand, pinch both sides of the loop right under the flower, then stretch the tail end and weave it randomly between the petals so it gets nicely stuck in place. Give the petals one last adjustment, and you're done!

Magic Wand

If you've made the Flower Bracelet, the Magic Wand will be a breeze.

You Need

- 1 balloon for the magic sparkle
- 1 balloon for the wand
- scissors

1 Make the magic sparkle by following steps 1–5 for the Flower Bracelet (page 34).

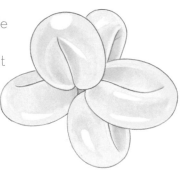

2 Blow up the wand balloon to about 18 inches (.5 m) long and tie it off. Tie another knot right at the end of the inflated part and cut off the uninflated balloon just below the knot.

3 Stretch the tied-off nozzle of the wand and wind it between a few different magic sparkle loops.

Adjust the sparkle so the loops are going every which way. Hand the wand to a kid and watch the magic happen.

Fairy Wings

You Need

- 1 balloon for the wings
- 2 balloons for the straps
- scissors

1 Fill the wings balloon nearly all the way so there is a scant quarter inch (.6 cm) of uninflated tip. Tie the balloon off and stretch it (pages 8–9).

2 Tie the nozzle to the tail in a double knot to make a big circle. You may have to squeeze the tail a bit to get enough uninflated balloon to tie to the nozzle.

3 Now find the midpoint of your circle by holding the tied-together ends in one hand and running your other hand along the length of the balloon to the bend. The bend is the midpoint.

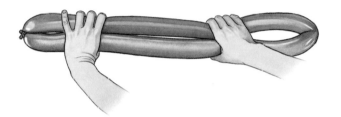

4 Bring the knot and the midpoint together, and twist three times. Wings!

5 Inflate one of the strap balloons all the way — but don't tie it off! Instead, let the air out so you have an empty, stretched-out balloon. Do the same with the other strap balloon and then tie them together securely at the nozzles.

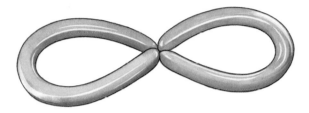

6 Set the knot in the center twist and pull the straps behind the wings, one at the top and one at the bottom.

7 Pull the straps snug. Behind the center twist, crisscross the straps and bring one up through the center of each wing.

Tie the ends together in a secure knot.

8 Set the knot in the center twist and pull each loop through the wings to the back.

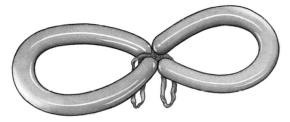

9 Run one of the loops through the other one...

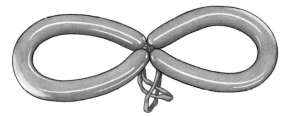

...and pull both loops through the wings to the front again. Done!

If you want more stretch in the straps, release any trapped air by cutting a little vertical slit in each one. Be careful not to cut the straps in two!

Your fairy will need some assistance getting into her wings, one arm in each strap, and adjusting them in the center of her back. Once the wings are in place, she'll be ready to take a solo flight.

Braided Wreath

You Need

- 3 balloons
- a cooperative kid's head
- scissors

1 Inflate the balloons so each has an inch or two (about 4.5 cm) of uninflated tip. Tie the balloons off and stretch them (pages 8-9).

2 Line up all three balloons evenly and squeeze them together an inch (2.5 cm) or so below the nozzles.

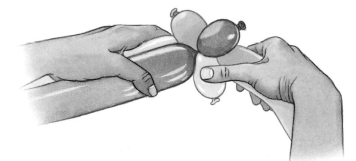

3 Twist them all together three times so you end up with three round bubbles.

4 To lock them together, push one of the bubbles around the twist and back to its original position.

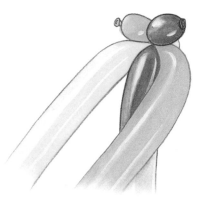

5 Now braid the three balloons: Starting right below the bubbles, cross the outside right balloon over the center balloon so it becomes the new center balloon.

6 Cross the outside left balloon over the center balloon — now *it's* the center balloon. Keep the braid nice and tight, with no gaps.

7 Keep braiding, alternately crossing the outside over the center, until you get to the end of at least one of the balloons. The braid will start to curl into a wreath shape.

Holding the end of the braid together, wrap the wreath around your kid's head and note where the ends meet.

8 Take the wreath off the head and twist the balloons all together three times right where they met the bubble end. If there was any braiding beyond that point, go ahead and let it unbraid.

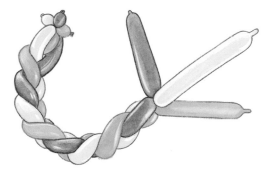

9 Form the braid into a circle so the bubble twist and the tail twist meet. Twist them all together three times.

10 Lock the twist by scrambling the bubbles and tails. Try to get each of them to switch places at least once.

Keep the long tails if your customer likes the look of them. Or use scissors to deflate the tails (see page 36), then trim them off or wrap them between the bubbles.

Bike

You Need

- 3 balloons for the bike
- 2 balloons for the wheels
- a little patience

1 Inflate all five balloons nearly completely, so they have hardly any uninflated tip at the end, tie them off, and stretch them (pages 8-9).

2 Take one of the three bike balloons and tie the nozzle to the tail in a double knot to make a big circle. You may have to squeeze the tail a bit to get enough uninflated balloon to tie to the nozzle.

Do the same thing with one of the other bike balloons. Now you've got two big circles.

3 Take the third bike balloon and bend it in half. Line up the ends evenly to make sure the sides are equal.

Twist the sides together three times about 6 inches (15 cm) from the bend.

Lock the twist by pulling one of the ends down through the center of the loop and then back to its original position. This is your first wheel holder.

4 Make another twist about 4 inches (10 cm) above the last one. Again, twist three times and lock the twist by pulling one end through the center.

5 Hold one of the big circles so the knot is right over the joint between the two loops.

Link the balloons by pushing the big circle behind the loop, with only its nozzle still in front.

6 Add the second big circle the same way, right at the same joint.

7 Hold the big circles in one hand, and all the rest of the balloons in the other hand, and give the joint three good twists to lock it.

BIKE ROUTE

8

Line up the two big circles. About 6 inches (15 cm) below the top, squeeze the sides together and twist three times.

9 You've just made two loops. One loop will form the back of the bike seat, and the other will be the back wheel holder. It doesn't matter which loop is which. Just keep twisting until the loops are positioned the way you like.

This next part is a little tricky and may take a couple of tries to get right. Take it slow and be patient!

These two loops should be about the same size.

10 Take one of the wheel balloons and rest the nozzle end inside one of the wheel-holder loops. Hold it in place with one hand, and use the other hand to thread the tail through the loop, on top of the nozzle.

11 Still holding the nozzle in place, pull the tail through the loop so it wraps tightly around itself like a cinnamon roll.

12 Keep wrapping and threading the tail through the top of the loop. Make the layers as tight as you can.

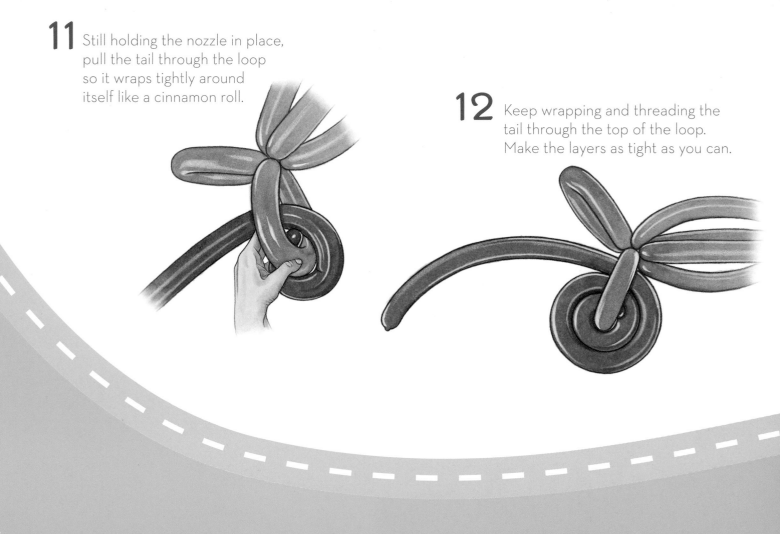

13

When the entire balloon is rolled up, hold all the layers of the wheel together and rotate the bike so the tail is held securely in place by the wheel holder.

Add the other wheel the same way.

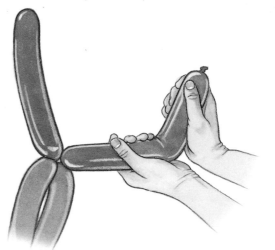

Bend and mush the handle bars to give them a handle bar-ish shape.

Done. Now hit the road!

Art Director Maria Corrales

Designer Keeli McCarthy

Technical Artists Darwen & Vally Hennings

Photographers Katrine Naleid, Peter Fox, John Cassidy

Photo Shoot Consultant Anne Schultz

Editorial Assistant Rebekah Lovato

Pop Stars Patty Morris, Barb Magnus

Big Bang Jen Mills

Totally Twisted David Avidor

Balloon Phobic John Cassidy

Special Thanks Pat Murphy, Escondido Elementary School, and all the balloon twist testers at Klutz

Models Jeanette Andrews, Soraya Chraibi, Jackson Clough, Laura DeMassa, Tyler DeMassa, Jacob Duran, Ehecatl, Shawn Ficocelli, Shelby Franklin, Nia Furman-McClure, Ben A. Gougler, Harper Goulden, David Grosshennig, Hanna Grosshennig, Emma Hammerson, Milan Hilde-Jones, Rachel Hsin, Naima Castañeda Isaac, Diavian James, Emma Johnston, Katelyn, Ally Lai, Brandon Lanesey, Gabrael Levine, Anayah Lillard, Emma Magnus, Alexis Massey, Patrick McEntee, Max Melnik, Jacob Mucciarone, Alys Olmstead, Olivia O'Farrell, Ezra Parkhill, Alexander J. Pereira, Carmen Pereña, Christopher Pierno, Misha Reswick, Niklas Risano, Ethan Rose, David Santana, Ella Schultz, Josefa Shea, Sophia Smith, Zoie K. Smith, Kim Spillane, Alyssa Bryant Sepulveda, Marissa Bryant Sepulveda, Annabel Su, Austin Tai, Olivia Tai, Justin Tang, Aidan Van Vleck, Alec Van Vleck, Jeffrey Ward, Isabel Wendin, Zoe Weiss, Julia Anne Schneider Willick, Rebecca Wong, Angus Yick

MORE GREAT BOOKS FROM KLUTZ

Face Painting

The Body Crayon Book

Cat's Cradle®

The Cootie Catcher Book

Fancy Friendship Bracelets

Lettering in Crazy Cool Quirky Style

Nail Art

Potholders and Other Loopy Projects

Scoubidou: A Book of Lanyard & Lacing

Twirled Paper

Window Art

BIG THANKS

to our Balloon Twisting Experts:
Megan "Dilly Dally" Murphy,
Raul Gonzales,
Michael "Funnybone" Ianneo

The Klutz Book of Balloon Twisting

by Karen Phillips

100% KLUTZ CERTIFIED

Caution: The Balloons On The Front Of This Book Contain Natural Rubber Latex, Which May Cause Allergic Reactions.